The Life & Times of Mr Pussy

THE LIFE
& TIMES
OF
MR PUSSY

A Memoir of
a Favourite Cat

THE GENTLE AUTHOR

Spitalfields Life
Books

First published in 2018 by Spitalfields Life Books Ltd

1

A CIP catalogue for this book is available from the
British Library

ISBN 978-0-9957401-2-9

A Spitalfields Life Book
Edited by The Gentle Author

Designed by David Pearson
Typeset in Chiswick Text Light

Printed by
Legatoria Editoriale Giovanni Olivotto Spa
Viale Dell'Industria 2
36100 Vicenza
Italy

Published by
Spitalfields Life Books Ltd
16 Victoria Cottages
Spitalfields
London E1 5AJ

www.spitalfieldslife.com
@thegentleauthor

I was always disparaging of those who doted over their pets, as if this apparent sentimentality were an indicator of some character flaw. That changed when I bought a cat, a couple of weeks after the death of my father. My mother was inconsolable and sat immobile for days. So I bought her a tiny black kitten in Mile End – no bigger than my hand – and I took him on the train to Devon, arriving late at night and entrusting him into her care.

At that moment, she was transformed from a woman with a bereavement problem to a woman with a cat problem. Looking back, I attribute Mr Pussy's placid and intelligent nature to those first impressionable months of his life with her. Six years later, after she died, he returned to live out his days with me in Spitalfields.

I now understand how pets become receptacles of memory and emotion, and I have learnt that this is why people can lavish such affection upon animals. Mr Pussy's age measured the time since I lost my father and, as he grew into maturity, my father's memory lived through him while his distinctive personality reflected my mother's own nature.

I held him in trust for her, and in love and memory of them both.

*

I think back to when I woke one night and decided to get a cat. It was a few weeks after my father died and I had been lying awake, devising ways to console my mother. The funeral was over but we both were still enveloped in crisis. I decided a cat was the answer, so I set out to find her one next day. Yet I hit a blank at once when I discovered that a cat cannot simply be bought at a pet shop. I spoke to cat charities and they could not help me either. They told me that an inspection of the prospective owner's house was required before they could even consider offering me a cat.

As a child, I owned a beloved grey tabby that I acquired when I began primary school and which died when I left home for college. The creature's existence spanned an era in the life of our family and, at the time, my mother said she would never replace it with another as its death caused her too much sadness. Yet I always wondered if this was, in fact, her response to my own departure, as her only child.

My father now gone, she lived alone in a large house with a long garden leading to an orchard. It was an ideal home for a cat, she had experience with cats, so I knew that at this moment of bereavement she needed a cat to bring fresh life into her world. I called her and discussed it, hypothetically. She told me she wanted a female.

I rang veterinary surgeries asking if they knew anyone giving kittens away, without any luck. Working systematically, I rang every pet shop in the London directory. One pet shop eventually offered to help me – as long as I could be discreet, they said. They had rescued a litter of kittens just a few weeks old, prematurely separated from their mother and abandoned on the street. These animals needed homes urgently. Naturally, the shop could not sell me one because that would be illegal, but maybe, they said, I could give them something to cover the costs of taking care of the others?

So I went to the pet shop in question, in a quiet street around the back of Mile End tube station. It was mid-afternoon and the light was fading. I was planning to go to Paddington directly from there and catch the train to Exeter. My heart was pounding as I approached the shop, my sense of loss channelled into this strange pursuit. On my right as I entered was a cage full of kittens, all tangled up playing together. Instantly, one left the litter and walked over to the grille, studying me. This was the moment. This was the cat. A mutual decision was made.

I asked the owner for the black one, now clawing at the mesh to hold my attention. The shopkeeper assured me the cat was female and, after a short negotiation, I gave him forty pounds. Becoming distressed when it was time for me to leave, "You will take care of it won't you?" he implored, tears dripping from his eyes.

Startled by this unexpected outburst, I quickly walked away and got onto the tube just as the rush hour began. The tiny creature in the box screamed insistently, drawing the attention of the entire carriage. It screamed all the way to Devon. I lay in bed that night clutching the little animal to my chest, as the only way I could find to lull it to sleep. My mother christened it Rosemary and the cat grew calm under her influence as she sat by the fireside reading novels through the long winter months.

The next summer, when it became clear that my mother could no longer live alone, I moved back to live with her in the house I grew up in. I discovered the new cat had fallen into all the same patterns of behaviour as my childhood tabby. Yet when we sent the cat to the vet to be neutered, there was a surprise. They rang to inform us it was a tom cat not a female. The name Rosemary was abandoned, instead we called him Mr Pussy in recognition of this early gender confusion.

I cared for my mother until she died, five years later. When the presence of a cat became too threatening for her in her paralysis, I had to keep Mr Pussy away from her room. He skulked around in disappointment and, revealing an independent spirit, ran wild, chasing moorhens through the water meadows of the River Exe. One day, I picked up Mr Pussy and sat him on my lap in the cabin of a removal truck and we made the return journey to London for good.

*

Mr Pussy sleeps at my feet every night, positioning himself like the dogs curled up at the feet of effigies on tombs. There is a sheepskin placed across the corner of the bed, his rightful place. When I roll over in the night, my feet meet the reassuring resistance of a solid mass, and I know it is Mr Pussy. He wakes at first light, climbs down and strolls along to the head of the bed, full of the joy of morning, and miaows in my face.

Commonly, I open my eyes to confront him eyeballing me at dawn, two golden eyes filling my field of vision. I turn my back on him, rolling over to sleep further. Yet Mr Pussy is full of delight to welcome the new day and cannot countenance my reluctance.

The first yowl usually wakes me from my slumber in the glimmering of daylight. If I should try to deny it, descending quickly back to my former depths of sleep, a louder, more insistent cry assures me that he will not be ignored.

Mr Pussy's disappointed response is to scratch half-heartedly upon the side of the bed, encouraging me to rise. I ignore him at my peril, as this will provoke him to walk to the end of the bed and scratch my toes sticking out from the sheet, causing me to wake with a cry of pain and pull up my knees against my chest in a defensive position beneath the covers.

Should I persist in feigning sleep, he will extend a claw and reach up to the bedside bookshelf, hooking my copy of *King Lear* by the spine and tugging it off in one stroke to crash down onto the floor, employing a particular choice of title that I have yet to understand.

This avenue now exhausted, Mr Pussy leaps in one bound onto the chest of drawers where I place my watch at night. The thunderous plonk of his landing always rouses me because I know what follows – a little tinkling, a little scraping and a little scratching, as he manoeuvres various objects in preparation for knocking them onto the floor.

As I lie there in half-slumber, I try to remember whether I left my phone upon the chest of drawers. I sit up to check and our eyes meet. Mr Pussy looks down at me accusingly, as he expects more than this sleepy-headed disinterest. Mr Pussy wants me to get up. "Pussy!" I yell in a melodramatic tone, throwing back the covers as if about to rise. He jumps down and runs from the room, eager to be the first into the bathroom. But I am too smart for him, I pull back the covers and return to sleep.

In weary exasperation, I open my eyes again momentarily to face his pitiful expression of need and my anger is quelled. The question arises: did I put out any food for Mr Pussy last night? In a half-awake moment of emotional vulnerability, the seed of doubt is sown. My sympathy is aroused for him, pleading for his rations whilst I indulge my luxuriant ease. Yet I am capable of indifference to his pain, rolling over in bed to seek another forty winks. In this case, experience has taught me that he will respond by running up the covers and leaping on my back with the agility of a mountain goat, so that he may yowl directly into my ear.

Thus, I have learned not to roll over. Instead, without opening my eyes, I extend a crooked forefinger in an attempt to pacify Mr Pussy through petting. Stroking him beneath his chin and on his brow provokes a loud and emotional purring and snakelike twisting of the neck. With a sound like an engine revving, Mr Pussy bares his teeth and rubs them up against my finger several times in glee. This causes him ecstatic delight and coats my finger in saliva. He may repeat the action several times with an accumulating sense of excitement, glorying in the moment, knowing it is only a matter of time before I accept that it is simpler to bow to his will than to resist.

Submitting to Mr Pussy's inexorable persuasion, I stumble into the kitchen and discover plenty of food in his dish, revealing that I have been played. His ruse was an exercise in pure manipulation, a power game. Too weary to recognise the humiliation I have suffered, I climb back into bed, put *King Lear* back on the shelf and resume my slumber.

When I wake hours later, Mr Pussy is stretched out on the quilt, oblivious to me rising. Yet if I should wake him, he stretches out in pleasure. He has every reason to feel secure, because each night he tests me and confirms his control. He can relax in the knowledge that he is training me to become obedient to his will, and in my weakness I comply.

Mr Pussy wants me to rise when he does, so he can follow me into the bathroom to lick the pools of water in the shower, then return to the bedroom to observe me dressing. Once this preparation is complete, he runs to the head of the stairs and pauses, preparing himself for the triumphant moment as we run down together to embrace the glorious morning.

*

I spend most days of the week alone in the house with my cat. When I am sitting writing, he likes to doze and thus offers undemanding company, savouring the quietude that reigns while I am composing my sentences. If I work in bed, he curls up on the covers so I can feel his weight pressing against me. If I write at my desk, he perches on an old stool with a seat of woven straw, attendant like a loyal secretary. If I sit beside the stove for warmth late at night, he stretches out to his greatest extent, until he resembles an animal-skin rug beside the hearth.

A modest creature, he draws pleasure from my company and I am always flattered when he seeks me out to rest nearby. He does not draw attention to himself – just the occasional shrill exclamation upon entering the house to announce his return, or a gentle tap of the paw upon my leg should I neglect to fill his dish. He positions himself at my feet during mealtimes as I settle in the wing chair to eat my dinner, tracing the air with his nose to ascertain the menu. Yet he is rarely insistent and, if I grant him a morsel or permit him to lick the plate, he will do no more than taste, since he is curious rather than greedy. His concern is not to satiate his appetite but to feel included.

Even if others are around, it is in the nature of writing that it is a solitary activity. A connoisseur of stillness and a creature of tact, Mr Pussy understands this instinctively. He lounges in silent reverie while I work, before falling asleep, snuffling quietly to himself. During these long afternoons of contemplation, my thoughts often turn to my mother and how the pattern of my day has come to reflect hers. Once she had finished the housework, she delighted to sit for hours reading a novel just as I settle down to write once the day's errands are accomplished – each of us enjoying the company of a cat.

I remember vividly how, when she was dying, she sought to make a reckoning of her life.

My mother was insistent that I must not doubt her love for me and for my father, forgiving the volatile nature that coloured the happiness of their marriage. "He couldn't help it," she admitted to me with a distracted frown. And then, quite unexpectedly, referring to the tabby that was my childhood pet, she said, "And the cat, she helped me, she was always with me." In that moment, I recalled how this creature followed her around each day as she did the housework that caused her such anxiety. I remembered how, returning from school, I once found her cradling it as she wept for her loneliness. It was twenty years before I presented her with another cat. In my mother's company, Mr Pussy grew accustomed to the afternoon routine, the empty house and the presence of one silently absorbed.

When the cat and I are alone in the stillness of the middle of the day, it is as if time stops. Mr Pussy seeks me out to share the passage of the hours before nightfall and I acquiesce, thankful for the peace that prevails in his company.

*

Mr Pussy may appear self-possessed, yet he is circumspect. He keeps a keen eye upon the life of the household and no detail escapes his attention. In spite of his sufficiency, domestic harmony is essential to his peace of mind. Like those lonely watchmen who once patrolled the city at night, he monitors the premises and the residents. He loves routine. He seeks regular confirmation that the rhythm of life is stable and ensures that his place in the household remains constant. He desires equilibrium and wants the world to be unchanging. He is the self-appointed guardian of the peace. He is assiduous and he sets an example. He is the model of poise and master of the subtle persuasion necessary to maintain the harmony he craves. He has his ways and means. He has ploys.

Mr Pussy wants me to be at home and stay at home. In his ideal world I would never stray beyond the house and the garden, for he does not. Everything he needs is here. This is the world. He cannot imagine what could be of interest beyond his personal utopia. Possessing a medieval mind-set, he thinks only the void lies beyond his known universe. Yet he is patient with my frequent absences. He waits.

Assuming the role of a sentinel, he settles down at a vantage point to pass the hours until my return. Innumerable times, I have turned the corner and seen him sitting there, a dark shape, waiting expectantly at the end of the alley. He will lift his head at the moment of recognition and, as I walk towards him, he will leap up and run to meet me, rubbing against my legs in greeting. Then he will step aside to clear the path and let me pass, following along like an escort or a shepherd. He will not accompany me into the house at once. He likes to see me go inside and shut the front door, so that he may savour the long-awaited homecoming, satisfied that all is well outside before entering through his flap and following me upstairs.

His favoured vantage point is the first floor windowsill on the street frontage, where he presides from above. If he is not immediately visible on my approach up the alley, I know that my gaze will be met by two golden eyes peering down at me inquisitively from the window. He appears at the top of the stairs when I enter the house, stretching his stiff limbs and peering at me curiously to assess my mood.

If I change my clothes and settle to open letters or read without paying attention, he will coax me from my preoccupation. His ploy is to remove my slippers by curling around them, gripping them in his claws and pulling them off.

Although delighting in frequent catnaps at regular intervals, Mr Pussy will not tolerate me sleeping beyond dawn because he wants me to conform to his timetable. Yet I discovered that if I lay a few sheets of paper upon the chair, he will accept this novelty as a concession, settle down upon the paper and grant me my wish for a few more hours of uninterrupted sleep. Thus peace is maintained and our domestic world runs smoothly.

*

I believe Mr Pussy thinks he is a dog. It all began with chewing my slippers. When I sit down in the wing chair to eat my supper next to the fire, it is Mr Pussy's custom to lie at my feet. I have learned to remove my slippers before he reaches for them. Mr Pussy grips one triumphantly, holding the toe in his front paws while kicking delightedly at the sole with his powerful back legs in the manner of a dog. Roused with excitement as the kicking accelerates, Mr Pussy flattens his ears, growls and turns to me with fierce eyes as if to say, "Look at me, I'm a dog!" Then he chews it.

The slipper business was the first of Mr Pussy's apparent canine traits. Since he became fully grown, people often exclaim, "He's so big, he looks like a dog!"

Mr Pussy likes humans because experience has taught him they pose no threat. Any stranger is another potential source of the adulation he needs to reinforce his ego. I cannot deny his tendency to show off. Mr Pussy likes to play to the camera. Give him a ball and he chases it up and down the house, bouncing it off the walls with the judgement and skill that indicates a simultaneous talent at both snooker and football – as long as there is an audience. He pauses now and again to touch up his grooming and make sure his spectators are giving him their full attention. Like a Premier League footballer, Mr Pussy possesses the killer combination of quick reflexes, powerful legs and vanity.

Perhaps the canine trait that I appreciate the most in Mr Pussy is his loyalty. He follows me around the house, runs at my ankles just like a dog and sleeps contentedly beside my desk all day while I write. Mr Pussy walks out with me whenever I leave the house, hoping to follow at my heels. He is always disappointed when I hasten my footsteps along the pavement to leave him behind. Mr Pussy does not understand why he cannot accompany me beyond Spitalfields and into the city as a dog would. He consoles himself with his daily patrol of the territory while I do my errands, but makes absolutely certain to be poised for an emotional reunion upon my return, bounding to greet me.

*

While Londoners luxuriate in the warmth of summer, Mr Pussy endures the hindrance of his fur coat, spending languorous days stretched out in a heat-induced stupor. As the sun reaches its zenith, his activity declines and he seeks the deep shadow, the cooling breeze and the bare wooden floor to stretch out and fall into a deep trance that can transport him far away from his physical being. Mr Pussy's refined nature is such that even these testing conditions provide an opportunity to show grace, transcending dreamy resignation to explore an area of meditation of which he is the supreme proponent.

He perches on the sill in the early morning and late afternoon, taking advantage of the draught through the house. With his aristocratic attitude, Mr Pussy seeks amusement in watching the passers-by below. He enjoys lapping water from his dish on the kitchen windowsill at the back of the house, where in the evenings he looks down upon the foxes gambolling in the yard.

Whereas in winter it is his custom to curl up in a ball to exclude draughts, in these balmy summer days he prefers to stretch out to maximise air flow around his body. There is familiar sequence to his actions, as particular as a sequence of poses in yoga. Finding a sympathetic location with the advantage of cross currents and shade from direct light, Mr Pussy will firstly sit to consider the suitability of the spot before rolling onto his side and releasing the muscles in his limbs, revealing that he is irrevocably set upon the path of total relaxation.

Delighting in this sensuous moment, Mr Pussy stretches out to his maximum length of over three feet. He curls his spine and splays his legs at angles, creating an impression of the frozen moment of a leap, just like a wooden horse on a fairground ride. Extending every muscle and toe, his glinting claws unsheathe and his eyes widen gleaming gold. The stretch reaches its full extent and subsides in the manner of a wave upon the ocean as Mr Pussy slackens his limbs to lie peacefully with heavy lids descending.

In this position, resembling a carcass on the floor, Mr Pussy can undertake his journey into dreams, revealed by his twitching eyelids and limbs as he runs through the dark forest of his feline subconscious where prey are to be found in abundance. Vulnerable as an infant, sometimes Mr Pussy cries to himself in his dream, an internal murmur of indeterminate emotion, evoking a mysterious fantasy that I will never be party to. It lies somewhere beyond thought or language. I can only wonder if his arcadia resembles Paolo Uccello's *The Hunt in the Forest* or whether it is closer to the water meadows of the River Exe, the location of his youthful safaris.

There is another stage, beyond dreams, apparent when Mr Pussy rolls onto his back with his front paws distended like a child in the womb, almost in prayer. His back legs splayed to either side, his head tilts back, his jaw loosens and his mouth opens a little, just enough to release his shallow breath – Mr Pussy is gone.

Silent and inanimate, he looks like a baby and yet very old at the same time. The heat relaxes Mr Pussy's connection to the world and he falls, letting himself go far away on a spiritual odyssey. He is somewhere deep and cool, out of his body, released from the fur coat at last.

Startled upon awakening from his trance like a deep-sea diver ascending too quickly, Mr Pussy squints at me as he regains consciousness, giving his brains a good shake. The heat of the day has subsided. Lolloping down the stairs, still loose-limbed, he strolls into the garden and takes a dust bath under a tree, spending the next hour washing it out and cleansing the sticky perspiration from his fur.

Regrettably, the climatic conditions that subdue Mr Pussy by day, also enliven him by night. At first light, when the dawn chorus commences, he calls to me. Having no choice but to rise, accepting his forceful invitation to appreciate the manifold joys of summer mornings in Spitalfields, I have come to accept that it is not an entirely unwelcome obligation.

I cast my eyes down to witness Mr Pussy biting the head off a tiny mouse on the living room carpet. With the headless body still twitching, I scoop it up with dustpan and brush, run downstairs and throw the remains outside where Mr Pussy consumes them all, skin, bones, feet and tail. Another day, I wake to the sound of him crunching the skull of a mouse between his teeth on the bedroom floor.

One daybreak, Mr Pussy wakes me in his usual manner, clawing and crying in delighted excitement. I stretch out my finger blindly. To my surprise, he does not lift up his head to meet my finger. Instead, my touch falls upon another furry surface, soft and silky yet curiously inanimate. I roll over and open my eyes to see a huge dead rat. Mr Pussy stands over it with a look of foolish pride like a game hunter in an old photograph. He has brought his fresh catch as a gift to share with me.

The forlorn carcass of the brown rat lies in the foetal position, looking strangely innocent with its fluffy pale belly like an abandoned soft toy, immaculately clean despite its reputation for filth. With its long teeth splayed at an angle, it is a sight that I wish I did not have to contemplate upon my bedroom floor at dawn. Especially as it was placed by Mr Pussy upon a pile of yesterday's clothing, giving the credible impression of sleeping there. Much to Mr Pussy's dismay, I dispatch the rat to the bin and throw the contaminated laundry into the basket. Then, to his surprise, I shut the bedroom door in his face and go back to sleep, ignoring his plaintive cries of exclusion.

I have to admit that Mr Pussy has a history of violence. In Devon, he killed regularly. I would often wake in the night to the sound of him chasing some poor creature around the house. I used to leap from my bed, shut him in another room and encourage the traumatised victim to escape into the garden. Even more distressing was finding injured birds for whom there was no hope. I am ashamed to confess that I once caught him with a snipe, although I did manage to rescue a huge moorhen with red feet that he carried half a mile from the river and brought in through his flap. It escaped to live another day. I know that Mr Pussy is just following his instinct and maybe even offering me a share of his spoils. Once, as I was setting up the Christmas tree, he brought in a mouse, laid it down in front of the tree and then chased it round and round the pot.

In Devon, Mr Pussy used to go roving for miles and return days later with a dead rabbit in his mouth. In Spitalfields, he commands an alley instead, walking up to anyone that comes along, scrutinising them in the manner of a guard dog before greeting them affectionately. He has traded the life of an explorer and wild game hunter for that of a greeter and security guard. I do wonder if this altered circumstance created his curiously hybrid nature.

Although Mr Pussy's urban life may be less exciting, I am relieved that he only catches vermin since he came to London, not birds. He may not be reformed, but much of the temptation has gone. Nowadays I must tolerate the small kills that satisfy his bloodlust in the hope that Mr Pussy's days of indiscriminate mass murder are over.

*

Mostly, Mr Pussy slumbers his hours away in the armchair that is his ultimate home, where I first laid him down as a tiny kitten and where he has spent more hours of his life than anywhere else. Even if it has moved two hundred miles from one end of the country to the other, it remains Mr Pussy's chair.

My mother bought the chair in 1963. She had been married five years, had a three-year-old child and was still struggling to furnish our house. She was patient, doing without and waiting until the opportunity arose to acquire suitable things. She had very little money to spend but wanted furniture that would last, and the passage of time has proved she chose wisely. I think she bought the chair in a sale. Although I do not know if it can truly be memory on my part, I can see her searching among the cut-price furniture in the shop, delighted to discover this handsome Queen Anne style wing chair within her budget.

It was a deep green velvet then. One of my earliest memories is of standing upon the seat, safe between the wings of the chair, attempting in vain to grasp the top. I yearned for the day when I would be tall enough to reach it, for then I would have grown up beyond my feeble toddler years. The chair seemed huge to me and I could crawl beneath it comfortably. This was much to my father's frustration when he sat in it on Saturday afternoons, attempting to take note of the football results from the television, completing his pools form to discover if he had become rich.

He never did, yet he never gave up hope of winning either. He sat in this chair filling in the football scores every Saturday, year after year, until he died. Just a few weeks after his funeral, a tiny creature slept curled up in the corner of the armchair, seeking security in its wide embrace. It was Mr Pussy's earliest nest. By now the green velvet had faded to a golden brown and the cushion had disintegrated, so that if a stranger were to visit and sit down quickly they would fall right through the seat. Yet this did not matter too much to us, as we kept the chair exclusively for the use of the cat who did not weigh very much.

To rejuvenate the chair, we eventually had a new seat cushion made and a loose fabric cover in a William Morris pattern of willow leaves, which is still serviceable more than ten years later. Once my mother began to lose her faculties in her final years, I often sat her in it so that she might benefit from its protection. When her balance failed her, she could not fall off onto the floor as she did from chairs without wings. After she died it became the cat's sole preserve, and it still delights me to see him there in the chair evoking earlier days. It is one of the last pieces of furniture I have from my childhood home and, although I do not choose to sit in it much myself, I keep it because I can still see my father sitting there doing his football pools or my mother perched to read the Sunday supplement.

One day I will have the armchair reupholstered in its original deep green velvet, but until then, by his presence, Mr Pussy guards the chair and the memories that it carries. I realise that Mr Pussy is keeping the chair warm for me and I am grateful to him for this service he offers so readily.

*

While other cats detest getting their feet wet, Mr Pussy loves water. He has never been discouraged by rain, even delighting to roll in the wet grass before coming into the house and shaking off the raindrops.

When Mr Pussy returns, soaked from the rain, I produce a towel and give him a rub down. He craves this, and will go out and get wet just to have the rub down afterwards, demanding this service with insistent miaowing.

Mr Pussy reminds me of the story of my father's ginger tom that he had before I was born. The cat once fell from the branch of an old oak at the bottom of our garden directly into the River Exe and swam confidently to the shore.

Realising Mr Pussy likes water, I give him towel baths in summer, to cool him when he languishes in the heat. Standing him on the garden table, I soak him with a wet flannel or sponge, give him a good brushing and then towel him down. The experience is powerful for him and sometimes his emotions get fixated on the brush, which he grasps in his paws with the same tender intensity that Elvis Presley grasped his microphone. Afterwards, he runs around the garden steaming in the heat before taking a deep sleep in the shade.

Although I am conscientious and leave him a daily dish of fresh water beside his bowl of dry biscuits, he prefers to drink rain or running water, seeking out puddles, ponds and dripping taps. Sometimes when I am soaking in the bath, he appears – leaping nimbly onto the rim – and cranes his long neck down, extending his pink tongue to lap up the bath water, licking his lips afterwards out of curiosity at the tangy, soapy flavour. When I stand in the bath to take a shower, he likes to jump in as I jump out to lap up the last rivulets before they vanish down the drain.

One day, I took the shower-head and left it lying on the floor of the bath, switching on the water briefly to wash away the soap in order to leave Mr Pussy clean water. Thus a new era began. He perched upon the rim of the bath, his eyes widening in fascination at the surge of water bouncing off the sides of the tub in criss-crossing currents. It has now become a custom, so he may leap onto the bath and manoeuvre himself down to lick up the racing trails before they disappear.

It was something I did occasionally to indulge him, then daily, yet now he demands it whenever he sees me – perhaps a dozen times yesterday and sometimes in the middle of the night too. The game begins with the spectacle of the surge of water coursing around the bath. Then, as soon as the water is switched off, he lets himself down head first, leaving his back legs on the rim and moving swiftly to slurp up the rivulets as they run. Each time it is a different challenge. The combination of quick thinking, nimble gymnastics and the opportunity for refreshment is endlessly compelling for him.

Since it gives him such euphoria, I cannot refuse his shrill requests, trilling like a songbird and indicating the bathroom with a deliberate twist of his neck.

From the moment I turn my steps in that direction he is ahead of me, leaping up and composing his thoughts upon the brink with the intensity of a diver before a contest. Hyper-alert when I switch on the tap, he is enraptured by the multiple spiralling streams of water and intricate possibilities for intervention. Running all the decisions in his mind, he may even make a move before the water is switched off. Unafraid to soak his feet, he places two paws down into the swirling current and starts to lap it up fast. Observing his skill and engagement as a credulous yet critical spectator of his sport, I cannot deny he is getting better at negotiating the bathtub and the runnels. His technique is definitely improving with practice.

Within a minute, the water has drained to trickles and, before I can rediscover my own purposes, he seeks a repeat performance of his new game – and thus, with these foolish pastimes, we spend our days and nights.

*

When the clouds hang heavy and the atmosphere is quiet, Mr Pussy divides his time between dozing on the bed and dozing under a bush. The pace of the city is stilled and Mr Pussy finds the climate conducive to resting.

Mr Pussy observes me with doleful eyes as I go about my daily tasks, too gracious to be overtly critical, yet he hopes that I might one day learn to appreciate the virtue of sitting peacefully for extended periods of time without other occupation, as he does. To this end, he waits patiently until a suitable opportunity when I am settled at my work before he approaches me. Arriving silently like a ghost, he reaches out a soft paw to stroke my forearm gently while I am writing, as a discreet gesture of companionship, drawing my attention without interrupting my activity.

Settling at my side and savouring the tranquillity of the hour, a purr of contentment emanates from him. If my concentration should wander from my page, searching for a word or casting around to seek the direction of my thought, then I chance upon his hypnotic golden eyes, meeting my gaze with their fathomless depth and opalescent gleam. He has my attention. He has an infinite capacity for staring. He knows I am a novice and he is an expert at it. He knows I cannot resist succumbing to his superior mesmeric powers. He has me spellbound and I share his stillness. The house is empty and we are alone. We look at each other eye to eye, without blinking, to see who flinches first.

Almost imperceptibly, Mr Pussy begins to lower his lids and I do the same. I follow along, as his supplicant. Our eyelids move in sync and we are nodding off to sleep, it seems. I might enter the feline realm, if I did not open my lids again momentarily – only to discover that his eyes are open too. It is a moment of mutual recognition. He was testing the quality of my will, exploring my susceptibility to mental control. He observes me. He is implacable and he wants me to follow his example. He knows how to be. He keeps himself and he seeks to be calm. He is always present in the moment. He is sufficient.

Equally, Mr Pussy is curious of me and the intriguing nature of my existence that revolves around things other than eating and sleeping. I am the object of his scrutiny, he is studying me. He is an anthropologist, living among those who are subject of his fascination. His research methods are unconventional. He thinks he may gain knowledge by osmosis if he sleeps close to me or he may imbibe understanding by lapping up my bathwater.

Not always an entirely conscientious student, Mr Pussy likes to contemplate his findings at length. He likes to sleep on it, and he is a grand master in the art of somnolence. He knows how to behave in these dog days.

*

After a time, when Mr Pussy woke me in the night by clawing at the bedclothes and crying out in the dark, I learned to pick him up and settle him down upon the sheepskin covering the end of the bed, where he would rest peacefully until morning.

Privately, I was relieved to have devised the solution to his nocturnal disturbances, calming his anxiety by exerting my authority as a human over an animal. Yet, over time, I found a new pattern has evolved in which he comes to the bedside and waits in anticipation. No longer jumping onto the covers to sleep as he once did, he now expects me to lift him up and pet him before he settles down to sleep. Unwittingly, I have become part of a new ritual in which he plays the part of the dependent child and I enact the role of the devoted parent, tucking him up at night. This realisation neatly relieves me of my complacency, returning me to the subtly troubling question of whether it is my cat or I that has the upper hand.

I cannot resist indulging his favour, since his motive is not duplicity but devotion. As he ages, his need for human contact grows. He strays less from the house, he stays closer and sleeps more, with a deeper abandon in his slumber. He has acquired a new sound, an ecstatic cooing that rises from deep inside. I wake to find him sitting upon my chest with his face inches from mine and he lets out this coo of delighted recognition. He looks at me with his deep golden eyes that are alert yet unknowing, seeking consolation.

These days he stretches out his right arm when he sleeps as if to get a better purchase upon existence or to prevent it slipping away while he dozes. The external world means less to him and he prefers peace over excitement. He is withdrawing yet seeking more ways to engage with me. Sometimes when he lies upon me, treating me as a human mattress, he reaches out his right paw in an unspecified exhortation.

I recognise I am his home and my vicinity is his safe place. Thus he takes great pleasure in the things I do for him as my reciprocation of his adoration. After dinner or when he is satiated with heat from lying by the iron stove, he desires to be let out from the room, sitting patiently by the door as an indicator. Once in the stairwell, he will settle upon a pile of paper bags that are conveniently placed to permit him to peer through the uncurtained window and observe life in the street outside. As soon as he tires of this, feels the chill and longs for heat once more, he will cry for re-admittance and I open the door again. Yet within ten minutes he may wish to go out again and return five minutes later, entering the room with one of his ecstatic cooing sounds – provoking my realisation that more pleasurable to him than the change of rooms is the opening of the door by yours truly. His prime delight is that I am his flunkey.

Just as when I settle him to sleep, he has drawn reassurance from my action and sought its repetition as a means to engage. He wants something from me, beyond food and shelter, and this is how he expresses it. This is why he reaches out his arm to me. Yet I am caught on the surface of things, encouraging him to be quiet so I can sleep or, playing the flunkey, letting him in and out of the door. I do my best to comply, but I do not understand his language and so I cannot answer the question he is asking of me.

*

On Midwinter's Night, the longest night of the year, Mr Pussy does not stir from the chimney corner. Warmed by the fire of burning pallets, he has no need of whisky to bring him solace through the dark hours. Instead, he frazzles his brain in a heat-induced trance.

Outside in the streets, Spitalfields lies under snow, the paths are coated in sheet ice and icicles hang from the gutters, but this spectacle holds no interest for Mr Pussy. Like the cavemen of ancient times, his sole fascination is with the mesmerising dance of flames in the grate. As the season descends towards its nadir in the plunging temperatures of the frozen byways, Mr Pussy falls into his own warm darkness of stupefaction at home.

Mr Pussy is getting old. The world is no longer new to him and his curiosity is now ameliorated by his love of sleeping. Once he was a brat in jet black, now he is a gentleman in a chenille velvet suit, with tufts of white hairs increasingly flecking his glossy pelt. Toward the end of summer I noticed he was getting skinny and discovered that his teeth had gone, which meant he could no longer crunch the hard biscuits that were always his delight. Extraordinarily, he made little protest at his starvation diet even as he lost weight through lack of food. Now I fill his dish with biscuits and top it up with water, so that he may satisfy his hunger by supping the resulting slush. Through this simple accommodation – plus a supplement of raw meat – his weight is restored to normal and he purrs in gratification while he eats again.

Once Mr Pussy was a wild rover, but now he does not step beyond the end of the alley and, in these sub-zero temperatures, only goes outside to do his necessary business. Sprinting up the stairs and calling impatiently outside the door of the living room, he is eager to return to the fireside and warm his cold toes afterwards, sore from scraping at the frost in the vain attempt to dig a hole in the frozen earth. Like a visionary poet, Mr Pussy has acquired a vivid internal life to insulate himself against the rigours of the world and, in the absence of sunlight, the fire provides his imaginative refuge, engendering a sublime reverie of peace and physical ease.

Yet Mr Pussy still loves to fight. If he hears cats screeching in the yard, he will race from the house to join the fray unless I can shut the door first. Even when he has been injured and comes back leaking blood from huge wounds, he appears quite unconcerned.

Only two small notches in his ears exist as permanent evidence of this violent tendency, although today I regularly check his brow for tell-tale scratches and recently he has acquired some deep bloody furrows that have caused swelling around his eyes. But I cannot stop him going out, even though it is a matter of concern to me that, as he ages and his reflexes lessen, he might get blinded one day and lose one of his soulful golden eyes. Since he is blissfully unaware of this possibility, I must take consolation from his response to the time when he could not eat, revealing that Mr Pussy has no expectations of life and consequently no fear of loss. His nature is to make his best accommodation to any exigency with grace.

Rest assured, Mr Pussy can still leap up onto the kitchen counter in a single bound. He can still bring in a live mouse from the garden when he pleases and delightedly crunch its skull between his jaws on the bedroom floor. If I work late into the night, he will still cry and tug on the bed sheets to waken me in the early morning to see the falling snow.

When I am alone here in the old house Mr Pussy is my sole companion, the perfect accomplice for a writer. When I take to my bed to keep warm while writing, he is always there as the silent assistant, curled into a ball upon the coverlet. As the years have gone by and Mr Pussy strays less from the house, I have grown accustomed to his constant presence. He has taught me that, rather than fear for his well-being, I need to embrace all the circumstances and seasons that life sends, just as he does.

*

I have rarely had an uninterrupted night's sleep recently. Although characteristically a mild and sedentary personality by day, Mr Pussy transforms at night into an insistent creature of voracious appetite, waking me from my slumber to demand that I feed him a nocturnal snack.

I feared there may be some sinister emerging affliction which might provoke this rapacious conduct, so I took him to the veterinary surgery for blood tests to discover any underlying problems. I was given a test tube to collect a urine sample.

When I returned home and released Mr Pussy from his basket, the challenge of obtaining a sample dawned. Dutifully, I tipped the non-absorbent granules I had been supplied into a litter tray and locked the cat flap, on the principle that once Mr Pussy did his business, I could syringe it up into the test tube. Yet this was not be. Instead, he paced around with increasing anxiety, taking no interest in the litter tray and seeking a likely location for when the pressure grew too much.

Mr Pussy chose the corner of the bedroom where the shoes are lined up as the smelliest spot in the house where his misdemeanour might be least noticed, and after enduring his vocal frustration for several hours, I was delighted when he squatted down beside my boots to relieve himself on the floor. "That's very professional," gasped the receptionist at the veterinary surgery when I delivered the test tube promptly, suggesting that I was perhaps not alone in my struggle with this particular task.

Once I had accommodated the painful realisation that Mr Pussy's recent nocturnal behaviour might signal his terminal decline, I received the call from the vet to inform me that all the tests revealed he was in exceptionally good health for a cat his age. He was a little underweight, I was told. The biscuits he had forsaken were high in protein and Mr Pussy is a large cat, so he needed to eat a significantly higher volume of other food to compensate.

The explanation was unavoidably simple. Mr Pussy woke me in the night because he had a ravenous appetite and I fed him too little. Now I leave him a generous late supper before I take to my bed and, thankfully, the nocturnal dramas have relented. We can all sleep peacefully again.

The short lives of domestic pets reflect upon our brief human existence and remind us of our own mortality, yet in spite of his age and his trials, Mr Pussy remains quick with life. When I lift him, he is alive with swift energy and lithe in motion. Every part of him full of vitality, he is conscious and present in the moment, paying absolute attention and wholly alert with all his senses. Mr Pussy soldiers on.

*

I woke in the small hours to the sound of a clock ticking. I walked through the dark rooms, mystified at the origin of this strange rhythmic beat in my house, which has no mechanical timepieces. I returned to my bedroom and discovered the source of the sound. In the manner of Captain Hook's crocodile, the ticking was coming from inside my old cat Mr Pussy. I squatted down to touch him where he lay, stretched out in the wing chair, and I discovered to my alarm that his breathing had become a harsh muscular spasm convulsing his body.

Next morning, his breathing softened and he lay stretched out in weary endurance upon the wooden floor. Occasionally, he would stand and change position. He would not eat but if I held a dish out to him he could lap up water and swallow it. I stroked his head and he purred at my touch.

Overcoming his lethargy, Mr Pussy walked to the window and took up his usual position, peering over the sill with pleasure at the wonder of sunlight upon leaves and the infinite minutiae of the living world.

It had been more than six months since I had an unbroken night's sleep. Consistently,

Mr Pussy woke me with his cries and overcame my resistance to wake and pay attention to him. As I arose, he ran from the bedroom, expecting me to follow, and either make his way to the kitchen or the front door. If it was the front door, I opened it even though he had his flap. Secure in the knowledge of my oversight, Mr Pussy took a wary look outside and, if all was clear, he wandered off into the night. If he led me to the kitchen, he sat by his dish and looked up at me in overstated expectancy, even if there was already food on his plate. Often, after I fed him, he followed me back to the bedroom and cried again. This charade may be repeated several times through the night until I could find some novelty to appease him – running water in the bath for him to lap up or discovering some for-gotten chicken liver in the fridge.

Sometimes, Mr Pussy just sat and cried at me. I could nor understand his night terrors. How I wished for words in those moments. As a last resort, I took him to bed and cuddled him against my chest, as I did when he was a small kitten, until he quietened.

Only once, I lost patience and shut the door to him, foolishly hoping that he could be silenced and I might get some sleep. His cries were vigorous enough to wake the entire street and, unwilling to risk complaints from my neighbours, I had no choice but to let him in again and resume our pitiful nocturnal ritual. In the morning Mr Pussy was peaceful, slumbering on the bed.

When I could, I slept late or took afternoon naps to recover. I was disappointed that I could not find a comfortable resolution, though I feared a resolution would come of its own accord before too long. Mr Pussy had been afflicted with anaemia for a while, although the precise cause of this was never diagnosed and medications proved to be of limited use against the inevitable.

Denying that he might not recover, I still had hope when I took him to the veterinary surgery that there might be a way to restore his breathing. Meanwhile, peering from the taxi window, Mr Pussy was overwhelmed with surprise at the vast spectacle of the city and its streets, a new vision of another universe revealed beyond his domestic existence.

Nothing could be done to extend Mr Pussy's life, improve his breathing or restore his being, and I gave my consent to end his days. The vet fitted a tube to Mr Pussy's leg and I sat on a chair next to the table where he stood to face death while still gasping for life. His body was strong but his internal organs failed him. Mr Pussy looked at me and I stroked his head as the vet administered a lethal dose of anaesthetic. I expected Mr Pussy to grow weary and fade out, but he crumpled immediately like a punctured balloon and the life was gone from him in an instant. His furry carcass lay dead at once upon the table.

*

Mr Pussy possessed a strength of spirit and presence of mind that never ceased to fascinate and inspire me. Equally, he spent every day of his life among humans and he studied them with his quick intelligence as a source of never-ending interest. It was a relationship of mutual curiosity.

How grateful I am that his deep golden eyes were undimmed until the end and the extraordinary softness of his black fur was never corrupted. Whenever I picked him up, I was always astonished by the miracle of his small lithe body, quivering alive. How I loved the honey-sweet fragrance of the short fur between his ears.

For sixteen years, through the travails of life, my cat Mr Pussy was with me. When my mother died, he consoled me. When I sold my childhood home and left, he travelled with me. When once I walked all night through the streets of London on Christmas Eve, he waited for my return. When I broke my arm and lay alone in bed shivering, he was beside me. Writing is a solitary activity but, as I sat working each day, through the long hours and the years, he was always at my side as a calm and patient presence. I could never be lonely while he was there.

I realise now that he was always in the periphery of my vision and, even now that he is gone, he remains in the margin of my sight. It will be a while before he fades from my familiar expectation. I hear sounds in the house and attribute them to him without thinking. Thanks to the reflex of my unconscious recognition, any deep shadow or dark shape I spy transforms itself into him. Even now, I expect him to enter the room or to come upon him in any of his familiar spots. Yet he is not here and his favourite places are vacant. Returning last night, I could not rest at home and left to wander the streets for an hour instead to calm my troubled spirits. The house had never felt so empty.

I cast my mind back through time. Exactly half a century has passed since I acquired my first cat, a grey female whom I simply named Pussy. For my birthday, I was given the right to choose a kitten from a litter born in the next street, shortly before I commenced preparatory school.

How curious, fifty years later, to be confronted with my former self, a lonely child delighted by a tiny kitten, and to appreciate – for the first time – my mother's motives in giving me a cat.

Although she never expressed it overtly to me, I realise now that she saw a pet as the solution to the loneliness of her only child. She encouraged me to read books and to write stories of my own too.

All these summers later, I sit here now alone after the death of my old cat and I am grateful for this recognition of her concern and kindness to me, newly granted. Writing has filled my life and I understand how this moment today is the outcome of that earlier moment, almost a lifetime ago, when the world was a different place and I was a different person too. It was the first moment when a cat came along to guide me, leading me on the long journey, through time to the moment of writing these words.

Mr Pussy was fine creature and he lived a fine life.

Mr Pussy was my cat.

How I miss him now I mourn him.

Mr Pussy did not measure his life in minutes, hours, weeks and years.

Mr Pussy did not count time as humans do.

Mr Pussy did not think of mortality.

Mr Pussy required no metaphysics because he always existed in his own feline eternity.

Acknowledgements

This book was published with the generous support of the following readers of Spitalfields Life: Clifford & Fiona Atkins, Graham Barker, Roxy Beaujolais, Jill Browne, Tamara Cartwright Loebl, Charlie De Wet, Keith Evans, John Gillman & Mary Winch, Libby Hall, Mark Hamsher & Elna Jacobs, Carolyn Hirst, Jane Jackson, Terry Jasper, Stella Herbert, Michael Keating, Hilda Keen, Bernard Lamb, Mark, Ann Marie & Joseph Loveland, Pat Lowe, Julia Meadows, Robert Medcalfe, Angus Murray, Ros Niblett, Jan O'Brien, Delamain Ogilby Ltd, Sian Phillips, Tim Sayer, Aubrey Silkoff, Larry & Linda Spivack, Penelope Thompson, Gillian Tindall, Robert Welham, Jane Williamson, Jill Wilson, Derek Wood and Julian Woodford.

I am grateful for the assistance of Rachel Blaylock, Sydney Diack, Walter Donohue, Ros Niblett and Tim Sayer who gave invaluable comments on this manuscript.

Also published by Spitalfields Life Books

Travellers Children in London Fields
Colin O'Brien

The Gentle Author's London Album

Brick Lane Phil Maxwell

Underground Bob Mazzer

Spitalfields Nippers Horace Warner

London Life Colin O'Brien

Baddeley Brothers

The Gentle Author's Cries of London

East End John Claridge

The Boss of Bethnal Green Julian Woodford

A Hoxton Childhood & The Years After
A. S. Jasper

East End Vernacular

Maps of London & Beyond Adam Dant